The long and winding railroad – in its heyday, the Overhead Railway was a great boost to the city's economy

A CITY OF FIRSTS

Liverpool can hold claim to that title when you look at the six and a half mile line known as the Overhead Railway.

A tramway inspector and driver stroll across the Pier Head deep in conversation – this photo dates between the 1893 opening of the Liverpool Overhead Railway and the 1901 tramway electrification

LIVERPUDLIANS would call it many things – the Ovee, or the one that still remains 100 years on, the Docker's Umbrella.

It was the world's first electric elevated railway. The first railway to use an escalator. Britain's first automatic semaphore signals. The first colour signalling lights. The list goes on – but the Overhead Railway didn't and is now a distant memory, much loved and much missed.

It was, in its hey day, a great boost to Liverpool's booming port economy. It also made the city stand out. Why? Because it was a Liverpool character in its own right. It carried manpower and goods to and from the thriving docks and also it brought white collar workers to the city centre. By 1919 – a year after the end of World War I – the Overhead Railway carried an estimated 22 million passengers a year,

that equated to 57,000 travelling on the system. The clattering of the train on the steel decking of the Ovee, as they passed above 16 feet high, became a soundtrack to everyday life for the next three and half decades. The railway was part of the sight and sounds of the early 20th century Liverpool. But, in the end, time and progress waits for no one.

The Overhead Railway is now immortalised in the magnificent Museum of Liverpool with an original carriage for all those who want to know how high it was off the ground and just what it must have felt like being on it.

New York, Chicago, Shanghai and many other world-famous cities have seen overhead or elevated railways in action. But Liverpool got there first.

We won't see its likes again – but it will never be forgotten.

CONTENTS

Trinity Mirror Media

Compiled by:
Peter Grant
Design & Production:
Zoe Bevan, Vicky Andrews
Cover Design:
Graeme Helliwell
Liverpool Daily Post & Echo Image Archive:
Brian Johnston

Pictures copyright Liverpool Daily Post & Echo,
Liverpool Records Office

Special thanks to National Museums Liverpool

Business Development Director: Mark Dickinson
Executive Editor: Ken Rogers
Senior Editor: Steve Hanrahan
Editor: Paul Dove
Senior Art Editor: Rick Cooke
Trinity Mirror Media Marketing Executive: Claire Brown
Sales and Marketing Manager: Elizabeth Morgan
Sales and Marketing Assistant: Karen Cadman

Printed by PCP

ISBN 978-1-906802-72-1

Shadows of the past – the railway was a twin parallel ribbon of gleaming, airborne steel striding along the edge of the waterfront, and known affectionately by all as 'The Dockers' Umbrella'

Liverpool's Dock Road in 1919

THE DREAM BEGINS

Even by today's standards, it was an impressively forward-thinking plan. The birth of the Liverpool Overhead Railway demonstrated just how ambitious the city was in the 19th century.

THE introduction of a rapid transit system for the masses was nothing short of pioneering.

Liverpool had grown to become the British Empire's second city and its docks were booming with millions of tons of trade from around the world.

Such was the volume of goods arriving at the port of Liverpool that the roads in and around the rapidly expanding docks soon became gridlocked.

The city's vision was a simple but brilliant one – new electrically-powered trains would snake along the waterfront, feeding the bustling docks with vital labour. With the tracks built on columns 16 feet above the roads, the trains' progress would go unhindered by the painfully slow horse-drawn carts that packed the Dock Road below.

And so was born the world's first elevated electric railway. It was a remarkable feat of engineering and an ingenious solution to the problem of rapidly moving labour along a Dock Road which was already choked with goods traffic.

A public transport scheme to serve the busy waterfront and city centre had first been mooted in the 1850s, yet nothing constructive appeared. But with the later expansion of the docks to the north and south and the increasing congestion of the roads, the plans for a rail network were revised.

A proposal for a steam-powered line operated by the Mersey Docks and Harbour Board was initially put forward around 1878. When concerns were raised about whether the railway was outside the MDHB's usual activities, talks were opened with interested parties from the city's business community. ➤

Liverpool "Overhead Railway
"Ives" Patent Gantry for Building Ry.

Drawn to a world first – the opening of
the Overhead Railway in 1893 is reported
by the Illustrated London News

WATER STREET

NOTICE

The Liverpool Overhead Railway Company was formed and leased the relevant property from the MDHB. The company's decision to switch to electric power was a brave one, as electric trains were very much in their infancy.

It was less than a decade since an experimental electric railway was exhibited in Germany. The only such powered lines in the British Isles, at Brighton and Northern Ireland, were erratic.

But the company pressed ahead with electric traction amid concerns that sparks, cinders and hot oil from conventional steam engines would fall on to road users below. There was also a need to keep axle-loads to a minimum. Construction on the railway began in 1888, overseen by the engineer Sir Douglas Fox. The line was built in mid-air, the structure and workforce supported on a special jig that moved along the route as the track was assembled piece by piece.

The waterproof, corrugated iron decking on which the lines were placed gave rise to the railway's popular nickname – the Dockers' Umbrella.

At four places along the line, opening bridges had to be constructed to allow ground traffic to cross through the network. The first stretch was completed in January 1893 and featured 15 stations, which were an average of 760 yards apart.

Trials began that month and the formal opening took place on February 4. The ceremony was conducted by the then Prime Minister Lord Salisbury, his presence a sign of the fascination the rest of the country held for Liverpool's technical achievement.

The railway opened to the public on March 6, 1893, with services covering a five-mile stretch between Alexandra Dock and Herculaneum Dock. The following year, the track was extended to Seaforth Sands. The Dingle terminus followed in 1896, completing the six and a half mile line.

Besides the cargo moving workforce, the LOR was used by ship repairers and a myriad of people taking paperwork between ships, offices and the Custom House.

Amid the grime and gloom, it was a twin parallel ribbon of gleaming, airborne steel striding along the edge of Liverpool's lengthy waterfront.

No other city in Britain had such a spectacular urban transport system with electric trains rattling along some 20ft up in the air above the streets.

It may be true that elevated railways had already appeared in some American cities, but these featured steam locomotives. And although electrically-powered trains began running in London from 1890, these were on a tube line.

Liverpool's railway was the first in the world to be both elevated and electrically-powered.

The Pier Head when the LOR was still young. The Mersey Docks and Harbour Board building, which was opened in 1907, is still under construction (top left) and horse-drawn wagons rumble along the dock road. Below, a Liverpool strike convoy follows the route of the Overhead Railway down the Dock Road in 1911

Landing stage and Overhead Railway, Liverpool.

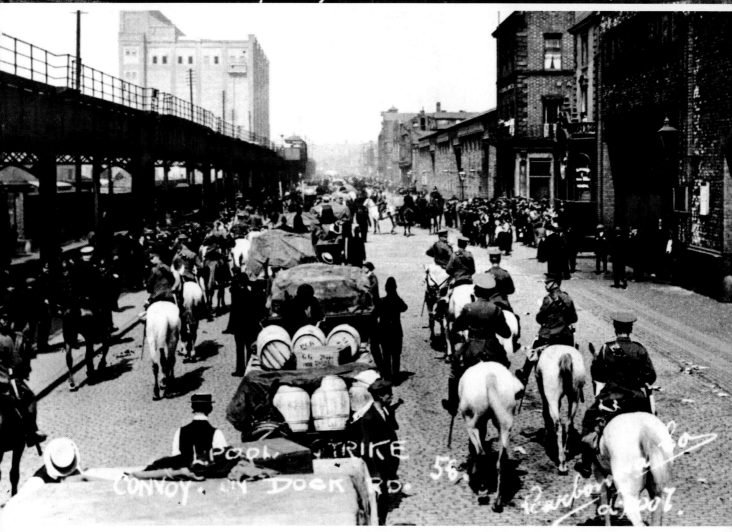

LPOOL STRIKE
CONVOY ON DOCK RD. 58.

View of the Pier Head in 1919 showing the Overhead Railway
and queues for the luggage boats on the River Mersey

April 1934 and the Ovee passes over the New Quay entrance of the tunnel as ticket machines are tested as a new way for drivers to pay tolls. Above, a train passes by the Liver Building at the Pier Head

A tram waits while an engine passes along the
rail track underneath the Overhead Railway

A RIVETING STORY OF A TRUE PIONEER

The Overhead Railway is most fondly remembered in its earlier years as a proud statement of Liverpool's ambition, boasting a number of technical innovations.

THE Liverpool Overhead Railway was a true pioneer and preceded similar networks in the US, again emphasising Liverpool's apartness as "Britain's North American city", sharing more in common with places across the Atlantic than others down the road.

Although it was under seven miles long, the LOR was epoch-making. It was held in profound affection here because it was so unusual and unique.

It was the world's first electric overhead railway – and Manchester didn't have one.

A unique method of construction was used which was designed to avoid interference with the Dock Road traffic. It was a fantastic piece of engineering, reflecting the great skills of the Victorian designers and engineers. After the supporting structure had been built, girders and flooring were placed and riveted into position by means of a travelling gantry on legs, the front pair moving on rails while the short back legs travelled along the section of viaduct which had already been built.

The gantry was designed by engineer Edward William Ives. Using the Ives' method, as many as 12 spans of flooring, each measuring between 50 and 70 feet, were fixed into position in just 5 days.

At Stanley Dock a double-decked hydraulic swing bridge enabled ships to pass through to the dock and at Langton, Sandon and Brunswick Docks to permit the passage of high loads.

The company's only steam locomotive, a Kitson steam tank engine known as 'Lively Polly' was in use from the inception of the line until 1947. ➤

The engineering project in progress

The station for Gladstone Dock, opened in 1930

Right, the Kitson engine used for moving men and materials as well as clearing ice from the rails. It was nicknamed Lively Polly by the staff and sold in 1948, having been replaced by a Rushton diesel in 1947

"The Overhead Railway was held in profound affection because it was so unusual and unique"

Interior shot taken in 1947 showing staff on board a carriage with the infamous wooden seats

"It was the world's first electric overhead railway – and Manchester didn't have one"

The trains each consisted of two motor coaches with room for 16 first-class and 40 third-class passengers. Each coach was powered by a pair of 60 horsepower motors and had an average speed of 13mph.

Later trains featured two third-class motor coaches with a first-class trailer behind them, able to carry a total of more than 140 people. At the turn of the century competition from the city's electrified trams saw the journey time between Dingle and Seaforth cut to 22 minutes from 32. This was later amended to 28 minutes because of the adverse impact the powerful 100 horse power motors were having on the railway's running costs. In 1901, due to competition from Liverpool Corporation's trams, a five-minute service was introduced, with 10 minutes between trains in the slack hours.

Due to the line of the railway following the contours of the dock estate, nearly one fifth of the railway was on curved track, which led to considerable wear to the train wheels.

This problem was overcome by a pioneering system of automatic lubrication developed by the then engineer and general manager of the Overhead Railway, Mr E J Neachell. Automatic semaphore signalling, using power from the third rail, was used for the first time, long before its use anywhere else. It was replaced by colour light signals in 1921.

It featured one of the first escalators in the country and was the first railway to feature such a 'moving staircase.' The 'Reno' escalator at Seaforth Sands station was proudly unveiled in 1901. However, it was short-lived and had to be removed five years later because ladies were constantly snagging their long skirts in the contraption.

The trains each consisted of two motor coaches with room for 16 first-class passengers and 40 third-class passengers. Later trains featured two third-class motor coaches with a first-class trailer behind them, able to carry a total of more than 140 people

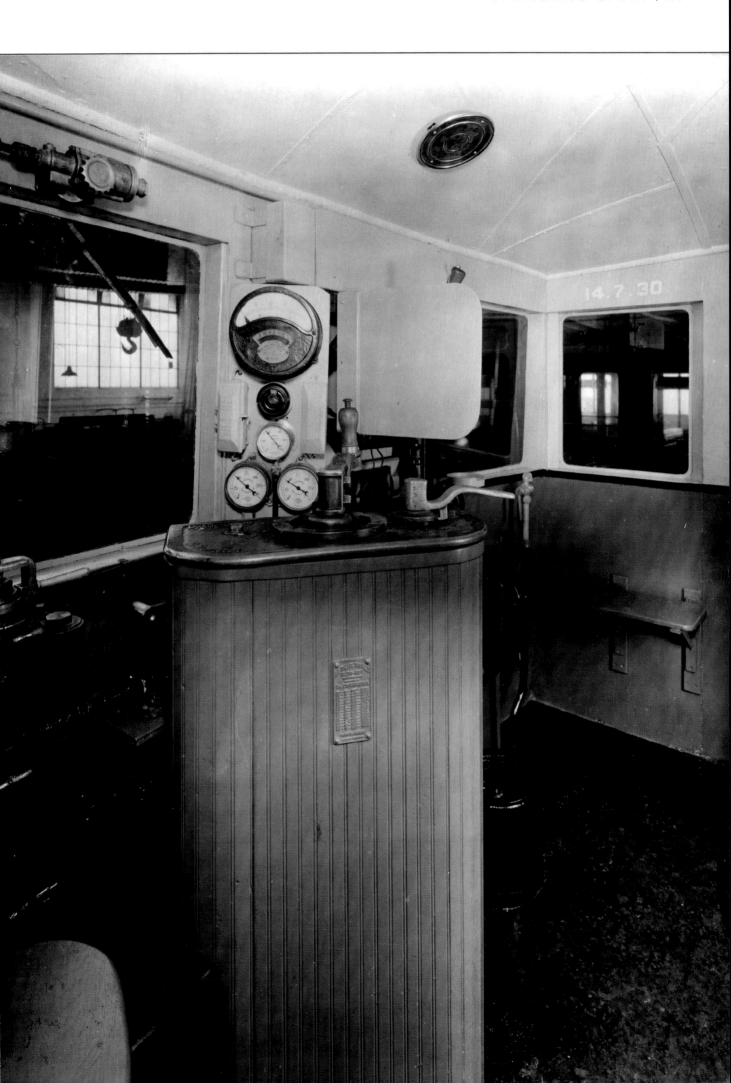

13 MILES
ROUND TRIP
1/8ᴰ FIRST CLASS   1/4ᴰ THIRD CLASS
CHILDREN UNDER 14 YEARS HALF FARE

MAP of the LIVERPOO
THE PRINCIPAL BUILD

RIVER

STATION TO STATION

*Join us on a Magical History Tour to discover what it would have
been like to travel on the Overhead Railway . . .*

THE Overhead Railway stretched from Seaforth in the North to Dingle in the South.

It served one of the busiest ports in the world, the centre of the country's economic activity.

Construction of the railway was a brilliant technical achievement, way ahead of its time and it was the first elevated railway in the world to use electrical traction. The LOR was custom built to serve specific areas of the docks. And some of the stations were only mere yards apart.

SEAFORTH SANDS

Opened after the completion of the railway's Northern extension on April 30, 1894 – just a year after the official opening. It was the line's most northerly station, and following the opening of the Lancashire and Yorkshire's company and Litherland station in July 1905, it offered a route to Southport.

It was located where the then Fort Road and Crosby Road South met and had the distinction of having a moving escalator, installed in 1901.

GLADSTONE DOCK

Opened on July 16, 1930 and the last to be built on the LOR, serving the dock of the same name. It was badly damaged in the Blitz but with sheer determination and spirit it was rebuilt and restored to service. It was situated at the junction of Grove Road and Regent Road. The dock served the transatlantic passenger liners.

ALEXANDRA DOCK

One of the original stations when it opened. Before the extension in Seaforth Sands, AD was the most northerly station on the line. It was situated outside Alexandra Branch Line No 2 between the Strand Road and Church Street junctions with Regent Road.

AD was itself by far the largest in the Liverpool system – the basin covering nearly 18 acres.

BROCKLEBANK DOCK

Situated at the bottom of Miller's Bridge in Bootle. One of the original stations, it was 696 yards from Alexandra Dock.

After the closure of Langton Dock station in 1906 it was very busy and used by tradesmen, labourers and dockers all working the ships in the Langton Graving Docks.

CANADA DOCK

It suffered heavy damage in a German bombing raid in December 1940. The track, just south of the station, received a direct hit, resulting in the loss of two crucial spans of track. It was soon restored to full operation.

One of the 11 original stations, it was situated near the junction of Bankfield Street and Regent Road outside Canada Branch Dock No 1. It was originally constructed for transatlantic passenger traffic, but later the dock became the centre of the timber trade with Canada and the United States.

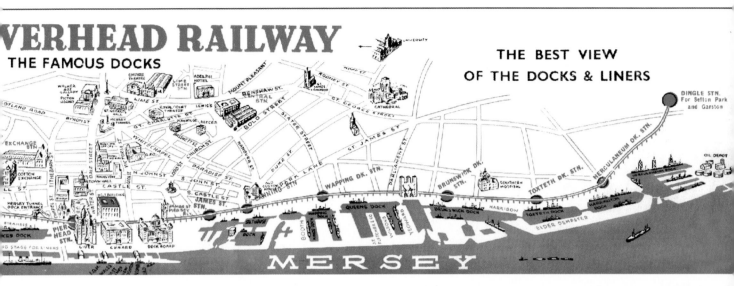

VERHEAD RAILWAY
THE FAMOUS DOCKS

THE BEST VIEW
OF THE DOCKS & LINERS

MERSEY

Seaforth Sands pictured in November 1956. The building on the platform is newly built, its predecessor having been engulfed in a fire in February. The station was not to survive for much longer though and was demolished with the rest of the railway in 1957

HUSKISSON DOCK

Built in 1896 as one of the two stations which replaced Sandon. It was another of the northern docks, used for the big passenger liners, being the main berth for the Cunard and Ellerman Lines and a popular viewing spot for those savouring the magic of the railway.

NELSON DOCK

Along with Huskisson Dock, one of the two stations built in 1896 to replace Sandon, reflecting the changing patterns of trade in this area. The station stood on the top of a steep incline between the junction of Blackstone Street and Water Street with Regent Road.

The 1 in 80 rise acted as a natural brake for trains on the 'UP' line.

CLARENCE DOCK

Another of the eleven original stations serving Clarence, Collingwood, Salisbury and Stanley Docks.

It was situated on the corner of Saltney Street and Regent Road and used by smaller vessels and so the station became an important stop on the LOR network.

PRINCES DOCK

The last dock, travelling south, before reaching the Pier Head and was one of the railway's original stations. It was located where Roberts Street meets Waterloo Road. Princes Dock had the longest floating landing stage in the world, used by thousands of passengers boarding liners, ferries, ships to Ireland and other coastal ports.

Canning Station

PIER HEAD

Probably the busiest of all the stations, providing a service for dockers and passengers making their way to the landing stages. It also served office workers in the city's bustling commercial area. The station was on the landward side of the Liver Buildings but long before the famous landmark was built. The Overhead was opened in 1893 while the Liver Buildings were not built until 1911. There was a magnificent bow-string bridge near the station which was an ideal site for advertising posters.

JAMES STREET

Located on the corner of Mann Island and Strand Street, opposite James Street and not far from the White Star Building at James Street station on the current Merseyrail network. It was the place where workers from the Corn Exchange, shipping offices and Harbourmaster's office would alight.

CUSTOM HOUSE

It served the huge Customs and Excise building in Canning Place – another original station. It stood at the junction of Strand Street and Canning Place, was damaged by the Luftwaffe in 1940 and, as a consequence, the Customs Office relocated. In 1945 the station was renamed Canning to avoid confusion.

WAPPING DOCK

Suffered bomb damage during World War II, it was located at the junction of Blundell Street and Chaloner Street. Wapping was just 806 yards beyond James Street and was the destination for those using the port's huge bonded warehouses. Now they are apartments, but what sights these buildings must have seen and heard.

BRUNSWICK DOCK

Another of the original stations built in 1893 and heavily bombed. It had a hydraulic lift bridge to enable a section of the track to be swung upwards to allow traffic carrying large loads to pass into the dock estate. Located at the junction of Hill Street and Sefton Street.

TOXTETH DOCK

Built in 1893 and situated near the junction of Park Street and Sefton Street, next to Cheshire Line's Brunswick goods station. The actual dock was later filled in and the reclaimed land used for building development.

HERCULANEUM DOCK

The LOR's original terminus on Sefton Street near the present day Brunswick Business Park.

However, when the southern extension was built in 1896 the original station was converted into a carriage shed and a new station built.

Just beyond the station there was a huge lattice girder bridge. The bridge carried the track to the tunnel which took the Overhead to the destination at Dingle. The tunnel was bored through sandstone with a clearance of just 33 inches above the existing Cheshire Line's St Michael's tunnel.

DINGLE

On the corner of famous Park Road and South Hill Grove was the southern terminus of the line following the extension in 1896. It was, according to researchers, more than half a mile inland, while the other stations were mainly parallel with the dock wall. The station was distinguished by the fact that it was the only station on the OR below street level.

The station at Canada Dock

Wapping Dock

Passengers head for a day at
the Grand National in 1952

SOMEWHERE OVER THE RAILWAY . . .

During its early years the Overhead Railway played a crucial role in Liverpool's booming port economy, transporting workers and sightseers to the docks and river.

THE Ovee's primary role was carrying manpower and goods to and from its thriving docks and white collar workers to the city centre offices.

The trains themselves contained a mix of third-class and first-class accommodation. Third-class passengers sat on wooden, slatted seats in a plain teak-panelled coach. Those travelling first-class in a separate carriage behind fared better, enjoying the relative comfort of upholstery.

The Overhead Railway was not used exclusively by dock and office workers – sightseers were also regular passengers on the service. From the outset, management at the Liverpool Overhead Railway Company were aware of its tourist potential, particularly as it was the world's first elevated electric railway. Early posters carried the slogans 'Affording Magnificent Panoramic Views' and 'A Splendid View

of the Docks and River'. Many a Merseysider can recall with fondness the sightseeing tours on this magnificent railway. It offered unmatched views of the docks and river.

In the late 19th and early 20th centuries, Liverpool was packed with stunning vessels, from tall sailing ships to great ocean liners such as the Mauretania.

Cheap round-trip tickets were bought for these sightseeing excursions and at certain points train users could get off the railway and view the ships.

The LOR company developed arrangements with the major shipping lines in which tickets were issued enabling its passengers to inspect the liners in the docks. Tens of thousands of people would flock to see the mighty ships in the summer months.

The mini tourist trade was also helped when, in 1905, a physical connection was installed at Seaforth, ➤

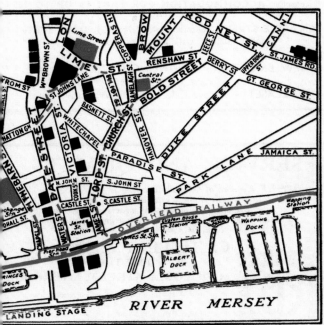

The Ovee flies through George's Dock in the early 20th century before the Liver Building was built

A clean sweep among busy traffic on The Strand for this worker

linking the Ovee to the London Midland and Scottish Railway main line, thus opening up a through-service to and from Southport. This was discontinued in 1914, when passengers heading for the popular Lancashire seaside resorts had to change trains at Seaforth.

In the post-World War II years, the need for a quick turn-around of vessels put a stop to rail passengers visiting the liners in dock. The LOR, by agreement with the Mersey Docks and Harbour Board, and in conjunction with an official Round Trip on the railway project, provided guides for conducting parties around the North End of the Dock system. This proved of tremendous educational interest judging by the number of schools from the Midlands and the North of England who regularly sent parties of children for this "geography lesson in Excelsis" a colourful phrase used by the general manager's office in 1949.

Even as late as 1955, the Ovee was still a massively popular and cheap form of transport, when a return fare from Dingle to the Pier Head was just six-and-a-half pence.

Greetings from Liverpool

Daniel Washington

Standing room only on this carriage in the 1950s

A TICKET TO RIDE

The Dockers' Umbrella is now long gone, but still fondly remembered by generations of Merseysiders, writes author Lew Baxter.

IT is, perhaps, quite odd that a railway structure built essentially as a means of transporting dock workers to their often backbreaking daily toil should still have a pull on the emotions of the people of Liverpool and the 'wilder' suburbs on both sides of the Mersey.

Years ago in the early 1980s, when editing the official Mersey Docks newspaper 'Port News', interviews with older dockers would usually at some stage turn into a nostalgic wander down the teeming quaysides and sheds of their misty recollections. And inevitably there would be mention of the Overhead.

I can recall often sitting and supping with a gang of old dockers in the Edinburgh Park Club that was their social hub and listening as they re-told each other tales of the Overhead and derring-do amidst the derricks.

"Ah, lad, it was a sad day when that closed. It was a part of our every day working life," many would murmur or words to that effect while enthusiastically pointing out where it had run in parallel to the fabled Dock Road.

It was, and is, a part of docks folklore but also of other Liverpudlians who used it for fun.
In the early 1950s Vera Fleming of Woolton, now 87, recalls taking her children off to Seaforth and Blundellsands for weekend days out.

With her cousin Molly they would gather up their broods and take the tram along Castle Street and down to the Overhead Railway station at the Pierhead.

"We would buy our tickets and then climb up the staircase to the platform. But usually we would also buy the kids a penny bar of Nestle's chocolate from the machines that were on the walls of the ticket office. There was also a bookshop at the bottom of the stairs where a man would be selling newspapers like the Echo. You could hear his loud voice as you approached calling out: "Echoa, Echoa." That was a familiar sound in those days.

"And the Overhead was the easiest and quickest way to get to Seaforth, which wasn't a big container base then," laughed Vera who also recalls that the carriages on the railway weren't comfortable at all.

"Well, they had wooden seats and were mainly for the dockers to get to work. We knew that so it didn't matter. And the carriages were painted a dreary dark brown, I think, and certainly weren't plush like todays trains," she said. They were very noisy also, as the train rattled along the rails. But it was great to look out and see the docks and river as we were so high up."

As a teenager Vera worked in a Liverpool office off Islington, as a shorthand typist and book-keeper, and would often walk through town to visit the shipping companies at the Pierhead to organise the despatch of her company's goods.

"The Overhead was a part of the Liverpool waterfront throughout my youth. We all knew it and loved it. But my fondest memories are those days out with the kids and using the train to get to the seashores of the Mersey. I still miss the Overhead."

Liverpool.

ARMS OF LIVER

Liverpoo

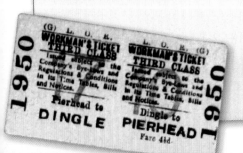

4148 L. O. R.
CUSTOM HOUSE
UP
EXCESS FARE 1½d. 4148

LIVERPOOL OVERHEAD RAILWAY
Canada Dock Station
R.M.S. "MAURETANIA" IN DOCK

"Many a Merseysider can recall **with fondness** the sightseeing tours on this magnificent railway"

L.O.R. THIRD CLASS PRIVILEGE TICKET.
(Series D)
Issued subject to conditions printed on back, and the Company's Bye-Laws & Regulations
AVAILABLE FOR ONE SINGLE JOURNEY
TO ANY STATION within 3 days of issue
Signature of holder
Date of issue
Rank   Issued by
0018

0162 L.O.R.
ONE DOG
Accompanied by Passenger at Owner's Risk
Issued subject to the Company's Bye-Laws and Regulations and Conditions in the Time Tables, Bills and Notices
PIERHEAD (L.O.R.) to

L. O. R.
ONE DOG
Accompanied by Passenger at Owner's Risk
Issued subject to the Company's Bye-Laws and Regulations and Conditions in the Time Tables, Bills and Notices
Pierhead to (L.O.R.)
Fare s. d. 0162

Overhead Railway and St Nicholas' Church,
Liverpool.

0648 (A) L.O.R. (A)
CHILD CHILD
Issued subject to the Company's Bye-Laws and Conditions in the Time Tables, Bills and Notices. Available
THIRD CLASS
Dingle to
SEAFORTH SANDS

Issued subject to the Company's Bye-Laws and Regulations & Conditions in the Time Tables, Bills and Notices.
THIRD CLASS
Seaforth Sands to
DINGLE
or any Intermediate Stn
Fare 5½d. 0648

Railway

"See Liverpool's magnificent docks and liners" boasts the
sign in this photograph by Edward Chambre Hardman

THE CENTRE OF THE STORM

The sprawl of the docks along the River Mersey was a major target for the Germans during World War II and the Overhead Railway sustained heavy damage during the Blitz.

MILLIONS of tonnes of war materials, food supplies and troops were passing through Liverpool.

Britain's war effort depended on the port remaining open, for it was by then the country's main trade route and lifeline. Its tactical importance led Liverpool to become the most bombed city outside London.

During the May Blitz of 1941, the city was hammered by the Luftwaffe during eighth months of terrifying air attacks. The raid claimed the lives of 1746 Merseysiders, with more than 1,400 in Liverpool alone. A further 1,154 were left seriously injured.

The bombings also left more than 51,000 people in Liverpool homeless and 25,000 in Bootle.

The LOR suffered heavy damage during the air raids.

From the vantage point of an enemy plane you could see the metallic snakes along the waterfront gliding 16ft in the air – the Ovee was in the firing line – only the two Liver Birds could warn them from atop the Liver Building.

But Liverpool and its people refused to bow to Hitler's onslaught and where possible the trains defiantly continued to run.

During the raids a number of stations were wrecked as result of their proximity to the docks. In particular James Street station was destroyed during the May Blitz and rebuilt on modern lines in 1942.

Canada Station was patched up after being hit on two occasions, before it was totally rebuilt four years later. Staff of the LOR were twice bombed out of their offices. When the railway was disrupted by bomb damage, a shuttle service using buses was called into action. The vehicles carried passengers to and from working sections of track where they could resume their train journeys. ➤

The Overhead Railway is brought crashing to earth near the Pier Head

During the May Blitz of 1941, Liverpool was hammered by the Luftwaffe during eight nights of terrifying air attacks

The Overhead Railway suffered heavy damage during the air raids. Snaking more than six miles along the waterfront and perched 16ft in the air, the Ovee was right in the firing line

"The **city** refused to bow to Hitler's **terror** and where possible the **trains defiantly continued to run**"

Even though there was a desperate need for steel and other raw resources for the war effort, the Overhead was considered so important to the workings of the port that every effort was made to provide enough metals to repair the railway after the air raids.

Thankfully and remarkably, no trains were lost to the bombers during the war, despite regular damage to the track and buildings along the entire length of the line.

Some raids took place at times of the day when the trains were still running, but even after the night service had ended, the coaches were still vulnerable standing in their depots.

The war placed a huge strain on the Ovee and all who worked on it, used it and loved it, with a massive rise in passengers stemming from the sheer volume of trade coming through the city's docks.

Astonishingly by 1945 it was carrying 14 million passengers, almost double the figure for 1939. When peace finally came most of the railway's ageing rolling stock needed repair or replacement.

Refurbished trains with a new body style began to appear in the years immediately after the war. The new look vehicles also boasted upholstered seating – to the relief of third class passengers who previously had to sit on wooden slatted benches.

Canada Dock station was patched up after being hit on two occasions, before it was totally rebuilt four years later

During the raids, a number of stations were wrecked as a result of their proximity to the docks. In particular, James Street station was destroyed during the May Blitz and rebuilt on modern lines in 1942

The station at Canada Dock takes a direct hit. Remarkably, no trains were lost to the bombers during the war, despite regular damage to the track and buildings along the entire length of the line

"The Overhead was considered so important to the workings of the port that every effort was made to provide enough metals to repair the railway after the air raids"

Last train to nowhere – the final Overhead
Railway train leaves Seaforth station in 1956

THE END OF THE LINE

The sad news that the Ovee was to close was broken to the people of Liverpool in February, 1955.

IT is ironic that what led to the Overhead Railway being christened the "Dockers' Umbrella" ultimately proved its downfall.

The steel decking on which the tracks rested certainly kept the rain off pedestrians underneath. But decades of exposure to the elements resulted in it developing serious corrosion. The decking's corrugated troughs were a natural water trap, inevitably leading to rust.

Repairs to bomb damage during the war revealed the extent of the problem, but priorities lay elsewhere during the conflict. When peacetime came, the decaying state of the Ovee could be ignored no longer.

As ex-worker James Mullin, of Norris Green, recalled: "You could stick a screwdriver through the decking, no problem. It was rotten. On one occasion I put my finger through it. It was just rust. It was only the big columns that kept the whole thing from falling down."

It was estimated that refurbishment would cost more than £2m, an impossible sum for a small private firm like the Liverpool Overhead Railway Company to find in the cash-strapped post-war years. Engineers reckoned the line could be patched up for £250,000, but even then it would last only another decade. City leaders began looking towards new bus and traffic improvements to provide the mainstay of Liverpool's public transport system.

Although the Ovee was carrying 10 million passengers a year and was still the city's cheapest form of transport, its days were numbered. With the nationalisation of Britain's railways in 1948, the Overhead found itself at a crossroads. If investment had been available, it could have become an important link in a wider public transport system. But as a short and isolated line, it was thought to be too parochial and insignificant for nationalisation. It was a line that ran from nowhere to nowhere and back again. ➤

Left, the track at Mann Island shows signs of wear and tear as the Liverpool Overhead Railway comes to a halt. Below, no turning back as the line is dismantled

The Overhead Railway's 70-year-old maintenance department steam loco, Polly – the first engine on the otherwise electrified line, used on a demolition train on September 30, 1957, nine months after the line closed

The Overhead's problem was that its fortunes were so closely tied to those of the docks it was built to serve. Liverpool's importance as a world port had begun to diminish, leading to cuts in the labour force, redundant warehouses and an overall shrinking of the dock infrastructure. Combined with escalating maintenance costs, it all proved too much for the privately-financed railway company.

In 1955, an 11th-hour bid was made to save the railway, as Merseyside's MPs met to discuss the implications that the closure would have on the workings of the docks. Local councillors and trade unionists also joined the public outcry. But the government turned down requests for a formal inquiry, arguing that passengers could be adequately carried by other means of transport. The then Transport minister, Harold Watkinson, also ruled that there would be no financial aid from the government to bail out the railway. At an extraordinary general meeting on July 25 that year, shareholders agreed to the closure and the winding up of the Liverpool Overhead Railway Company.

The final trains ran on December 30, 1956. The historic day was marked by many people turning out to take a last ride on what had long been regarded as a famous Liverpool landmark. ➤

"All the pubs along the route emptied and the people stood and waved as we passed by."

Driver Sutcliffe Fawcett was behind the controls of the last Overhead train to leave Dingle for Seaforth. At the same time, his colleague Jack Mackey set off in the opposite direction.

Stan Soudet, who worked in the ticket office at Seaforth on the final day, recalled: "I got the last train back to Dingle where I lived. There were quite a few passengers on board. All the pubs along the route emptied and the people stood and waved as we passed by. The driver blew the train's whistle back to them. It was a sad day. I had been working on the railway since I was 15. I had done every job there was to do, bar driver. The trains were always on time. They never broke down."

The demolition work began nine months later at the southern end of the line, close to the Herculaneum Dock. James Mullin worked for the Mersey Docks and Harbour Board, disconnecting the lighting system underneath the railway during the demolition. He recalled: "We worked on the section between Dingle and the Pier Head. We dismantled the lights under the Overhead, taking away the fuse boxes and cabling so the demolition crews would not be electrocuted. It was a pity it could not be repaired. The big support columns the railway rested on would have lasted until today."

Today there is precious little evidence remaining of the Overhead Railway's existence. The six-mile track and its supporting girders were scrapped as post-war Liverpool looked towards a bright new future. These days sightseers have to look hard to spot the few surviving pieces of the railway. A few columns rest in the walls of Wapping and Princes docks. The portal above the Dingle tunnel, bearing the inscription 'LOR Southern Extension' can also still be seen.

December 30, 1956 and Graham Page, Crosby MP,
thanks driver Sutcliffe Fawcett, after the arrival of the
last Overhead Railway train at Seaforth Station

Two way traffic, above and below, in the last days of the Ovee in April 1956. Dock Road congestion would return when the railway was demolished

Mind the gap – Herculaneum Bridge in 1956

The Overhead Railway had a heart of steel.
Below, Goodbye old friend . . . the station
and track at James Street comes down

Journey's End – this scene around the waters of Princes Dock, shows the
Overhead Railway surrounded by a warehouse world in August, 1956

The railway is dismantled at Liverpool's Herculaneum Dock

The Strand in Liverpool city centre in 1958, viewed from the Cunard building and showing the last arches of the dismantled Overhead Railway to the left, as well as St Nicholas Church and Tower Buildings

Some of the last remnants
of the Overhead Railway

"The **big** support columns the railway rested on would have **lasted until** today."

BACKTRACKING

The 'Overheard Railway' – memories of The Ovee . . .

Fred O'Brien
Historian

MY Dad often took me on the Overhead Railway when I was nine or ten-years-old. Several times, we went from terminus to terminus. It gave me a great view of the streets, but best of all was seeing Cunarders in dock and at Princes Dock station.

My mind may be playing tricks but I think I saw three in simultaneously. Those great ships like the Mauretania, Carinthia, Oriana, Queen Elizabeth, Reina del Mar, even relatively small ones such as the Accra, Apapa and suchlike. All were wonderful to behold.

I remember seeing huge steam locomotives built at the Vulcan Works, Newton le Willows being hoisted aboard freighters taking them to Peru, Bolivia, Venezuela, Canada and Australia. Titan was one of the floating cranes, one of three which were WWI German reparations. I wondered about the various destinations and thought I was just enjoying myself. Truth to tell, I was being educated. Thanks Dad.

By 1956, the whole raison d'etre of the Overhead was past, with rapidly-falling numbers of dockers and other factors contributing to its demise. There was another reason – a major design fault. Rainwater collected where the support pillars met the horizontal sections, leading to corrosion there. Demolition became inevitable.

I, for one, recall the Overhead with great affection and wish it was still here. Nostalgia may not be what it used to be but I do miss Liverpool Overhead Railway.

I was so moved to be able to see, feel and sit in an original LOR carriage in the Museum of Liverpool. The footage shot by the Lumieres in 1896 is there showing the scene from the driver's viewpoint. Says it all.

Stan Boardman
Entertainer

I WAS about 12 when I first remember the Overhead Railway. I was in a class of 40 kids – 4B Secondary Modern in Grant Road, Dovecot. The LOR was always popular with school parties. I can recall talking to the ever friendly dockers – seeing the Empress of Canada ship on its side in the dock, all burned out. I saw pictures in the Liverpool Echo so it was true. I won't forget that image. And the smells and the sights. We were, as kids, so high up and I could see all the docks, Birkenhead and New Brighton. It was a different world. Then I got up one morning and went into town and it had gone . . . gone forever. I don't think they should have demolished it. What a great tourist attraction it would have been in the modern Liverpool – past, present and future, all symbolised in the Ovee.

Billy Butler
Radio presenter

I USED to get the LOR on the way to work. I remember seeing all the ships when you looked out of the window. It was a bus to me – a functionary train ride to work. When I worked on the docks, I recall seeing the Empress of Canada – we all went to see that. In hindsight it's easy to say we should have kept it, but it would now be a great tourist attraction and ease the congestion on the Dock Road. But my biggest worry was always that King Kong, from the film, would sweep down and pick me up in the carriage. That still haunts me!

"It was a **seagull's view** of the docks and river – Liverpool's first helicopter **capturing the magic below**"
Ken Dodd

Ken Pye
Historian

IN its final year, when I was five-years-old, my mother took me for a trip along the full length of the Overhead Railway. She was determined that I should have the opportunity to travel 'On the Overhead' just once, before it disappeared forever. And I am very grateful for the experience.
 I clearly remember gazing down the docks as we clattered overhead; looking at what appeared to be hundreds of ships, sailing on the river and berthed in all the docks. I remember crowds and crowds of people, of all shapes and sizes and skin colours, walking the length of the Dock Road.
 I also remember the smells of the men who crowded the compartments, a reassuring smell to a small boy, of oil, sweat and Capstan full-strength cigarettes. I remember, too, the sounds of the strange accents from sailors from all over the world and the rattling and shaking of the wooden carriages as they trundled along the clanking and ringing metal track. Even today, the excitement and thrill of it all is a vivid memory.

Sam Leach
Author

WHAT an ear-splitting bounce of a trip. Hard wooden seats, which really were just cheap slats that were more like railway sleepers. The noise was terrible as you bounced around, trying not to fall off. Your bottom would be raw when you got off. But I was enjoying every minute of it. I looked at the world's shipping berthed in each dock with many more waiting on the Mersey Bar. Over 200 ships weekly, in those halcyon, exciting days. There were valiant efforts to resurrect the LOR, but the last train stopped in 1956. Days never to return . . .

A busy evening on the Overhead Railway in the 1950s – note the young lad in the centre who appears to have just realised he has forgotten something very important . . . too late

Frank Carlyle
Historian

IN my work as a lecturer in and around the city, I am often asked if I travelled on the Overhead Railway. Well, I always smile.
 Yes, I was lucky, because I actually did travel on it. And the memory has stayed with me to this very day. I recall travelling down on a bus to the Pier Head, going up lots of stairs to board this 'train in the sky'; passing lots and lots of ships berthed in the docks and disembarking at the point we boarded by the Liver Building. I do feel lucky travelling on one of the world's first iconic 'Superstructures.' So I can boast and am here to tell the tale of how I travelled on the L(S)OR – Legendary Superstructure Overhead Railway. There were many, many protests about its closure and equally many passionate attempts to save the Overhead Railway.
 Unfortunately, the decision was made to demolish it and in doing so leave an enormous void in Liverpool's great heritage.

Micky Finn
Comedian

IT'S ironic, I went on the Overhead Railway as a kid and here I am now at the Museum of Liverpool as a model with a cap on, pointing out of the window!
 I was proud to be part of it. I was never a docker using it as an umbrella but I saw plenty who did. I am grateful that I travelled on it and saw all the enjoyment it gave people.
 Imagine if it was here today? But now it has been brought back home to the place where it actually passed in its hey day.

"We won't
see or experience
its like again . . ."
*Letter to the Liverpool Echo,
1956*

The Pacific Navigation Company offices
watch over the Overhead Railway at
the foot of James Street in 1955

James Mullin
Norris Green

IT was part of our life, riding up and down the line. You would ride the railway as much as you would a tram car in those days. It was marvellous to ride on it. You could see right across the river and see all the ships in the docks. The activity on the docks was fascinating. As one ship was being pulled out of its berth by the tugs, another was sliding into its place. This was happening all over the docks. There were ships queuing up in Liverpool Bay to come into the river. The trains were quite comfortable and your journeys were normally very short anyway. Most dockers only travelled for a few stations.

John Bray
Dingle

THE railway was my first job at 16 and I served an apprenticeship as an engineer. My father Pat was a driver, he had been on the railway since he came out of the army after World War I, so that was what attracted me to it in the first place. I was only a lad, so I had to be supervised, but it was my job to check the signals, the lighting and the rails every day.

Even before the war, they had the safest signalling going. When a train came along, if the signal was red it used to trip and automatically put the brakes on. It meant there were never any accidents like there are today and it always ran on time, in all weathers.

Back then, people didn't just use it to commute, they came from miles just to see it. Even celebrities came to use it in its heyday. I remember once the actor Alistair Sim travelling on it just to get the best view of the docks.

Stan Soudet
West Derby

I STARTED as a carriage cleaner in February 1937, then I moved on to being an inspector and finally I was a booking clerk. The only job I didn't do was a driver, and that was because the war came along and I volunteered and joined the Navy.

In my first job, cleaning out the first and second class compartments, I'd start at either 6.30am or 3pm and I'd scrub the floor in the first class with Aunt Sally, a liquid soap, and then mop it out.

It was hard work but I really enjoyed it, because everyone working on the railway got on well with one another. I honestly couldn't pick the happiest time of my 20 years because every day was happy and I always looked forward to going to work.

We'd get snow on the rails and flashes from the live track but there were never any weather delays. The Overhead Railway was always very reliable, down to the minute. They ran every six minutes in peak hour and they were never late.

Frances Campbell
Conwy, North Wales

MY paternal grandfather, William Jackson, was an inspector at one of the stations when it first opened and then my father, William Arthur Jackson, became a guard on his return from World War I in 1918.

He then became a driver, and remained so until his death in the May Blitz of 1941, when our house in Wordsworth Street, Bootle, took a direct hit. It was my father's 48th birthday. Both my brothers, Jack and Harold, joined the Overhead straight from school, at the age of 14. They were still wearing shorts! Jack was a member of the plate-laying gang and Harold a guard. I recall, as a schoolgirl, taking Dad his lunch and travelling to the Dingle, then back to Seaforth Sands. What happy days!

My husband, Frank, also spent a few short weeks working on the railway before it closed in 1956. And myself and other family members then made the final sentimental journey – on the last train to run. I was pictured in the Liverpool Echo, holding the station cat from Seaforth Sands, a kitten which I gave a home and called Tibbs.

"I recall, as a schoolgirl, taking Dad his lunch and **travelling to Dingle**, then back to Seaforth Sands. **What happy days!**"

Writer Peter Grant is impressed with the sight of the original motor coach from the railway

COMING HOME

Between yesterday and today – by Peter Grant

I WAS often told about the Overhead Railway by my dad.

He was a docker. He had an emotional share in it since it was called the 'Dockers Umbrella'.

But there was much more to this unique piece of rail transport. When I heard a piece of history was being brought back to life I had to see it. To experience it and see what it must have been like travelling on it in its 60 or so glorious years.

And so, in 2011 I sat down in the wooden seats of the third class carriage of Motor Number 3, made in 1882. It is one of the original motor coaches which had electric motors mounted beneath the floor with a driving cab at one end.

It was one of the first batches of coaches built by Brown, Marshall and Company of Saltley, Birmingham.

It served on the Overhead Railway until it closed in 1956 and was preserved as the only example of a motor coach to survive.

It's been a sentimental journey for the motor coach, which moved from storage following the same route it took when it travelled the seven and a half mile distance along the length of Liverpool docks from 1893. The largest newly-built national museum to be built in Britain for more than a century, internal fit out of the galleries in the new Museum of Liverpool has begun, in preparation for the opening in 2011, and 'Coach No. 3' was the first object to be integrated into display.

Sharon Granville, executive director for the Museum of Liverpool said: "This is a momentous occasion for the project as the carriage - one of Liverpool's icons - is installed in the new museum.

"A lot of planning has gone into the display of the motor coach due to its sheer size, weight and rarity.

"The building has been designed to house this object and we have purposely left a large gap in the gallery wall in order to move the carriage in. It will then be lifted using hydraulics into an elevated position at the height it would have travelled when it was The Dockers' Umbrella."

The carriage – which weighs approximately 20 tonnes – is displayed as part of a reconstruction of Pier Head station, accompanied by Lumière Brothers' archive footage filmed from the Overhead Railway in 1897, to give visitors a real taste of what it was like to travel on it and realise the impact of Liverpool's port at that time.

'Carriage No. 3' will take its place above a gallery dedicated to telling the story of Liverpool's port history, and how the city transformed itself from a small tidal inlet into one of the world's greatest ports.

Presented to National Museums Liverpool after the Overhead Railway closed in 1956, it was one of the most popular exhibits in National Museums Liverpool's collection, on display in the Transport Gallery in the basement of what was the old Liverpool Museum (now World Museum) for many years. For the last ten years it has since been in conservation in preparation for display in the Museum of Liverpool.

Sharon Granville said with pride: "As the only surviving motor coach from the Liverpool Overhead Railway, our team has worked so hard on restoring the carriage to its former glory."

And so there I was sitting with the ghosts of yesteryear imagining what the world must have looked like more than 16 feet up in the sky. ➤

"As the only surviving motor coach from the railway, our team has worked so hard on restoring the carriage to its former glory"

The Overhead Railway gallery in the Museum of Liverpool tells the remarkable story of the first electric elevated railway in the world

I looked out of the window – the train wasn't moving but I felt moved. I imagined all the stations – from start to finish – that I have read so much about.

I imagined the ships below. I looked at the signs – 'Spitting Prohibited' – as if I would!

I looked around the exhibition. I smiled at the uniforms, whistles, keys, posters, maps and tickets of a bygone age. I listened to the voices, the interviews and the historians regaling the tales of what was and what might have been. I could hear the chatter of the travellers, people of all ages and the rattle and roll of this great piece of engineering. And I was a child again, as I looked at the magnificent scale model of the Overhead Railway where I could explore stations along the route. It was like being on a film set.

In fact, ever since the Lumiere Brothers filmed the Overhead Railway, it has not been camera shy, having featured in films, documentaries, books, songs, on artwork and even on YouTube.

It has appeared as a backdrop in the Ealing Studio film 'The Magnet', filmed in and around Merseyside. Award-winning Liverpool-born film director Terence Davies also highlights the LOR in his film 'Of Time and the City'. Atmospheric scenes of the famous landmark illustrate a bygone age.

The Dockers' Umbrella features on posters, mugs and all manner of memorabilia celebrating this iconic mode of travel. And with a nice touch of irony it is also featured in a stunning artwork – underground at Merseytravel's Moorfields station. Maghull artist Grant Searl created the image featuring the Overhead Railway with its Barker and Dobson advert.

"The timing of the film and the recreation of the Overhead Railway was just right"

Grant says: "I scanned loads of pictures but found what I wanted in images that captured the essential elements of a city – the Overhead Railway was, and still is, one of them."

More recently, the LOR has risen again as a celluloid hero in the film 'Charlie Noades RIP'. Written by and starring Neil Fitzmaurice, it was produced by his brother, Tony, and made right in Liverpool. The recreation using computer generated imagery

Tony and Neil Fitzmaurice (pictured below) worked with CGI specialist Steven Wheeler to recreate the Overhead Railway for the film 'Charlie Noades RIP'

(CGI) was a crucial element of the film, because Neil wanted the 1950s scenes to look as realistic as possible. He recalled: "We filmed in 2006 to coincide with the 50th anniversary of the closure of the railway. It opened in 1893 and became as much a landmark and institution as a practical asset for the city and its people. It also provided passengers with spectacular views of the city and its docks."

Tony Fitzmaurice looks back with pride and says: "The timing of the film and the recreation of the Overhead Railway was just right.

"The film was generally set in the modern day – we could easily have relied on archive footage when going back to the 1950s but we wanted to get as close as we could to the feel and atmosphere of that era.

"We knew it was worth taking the time and trouble because it meant a lot to many people in Liverpool."

And the man in charge of painstakingly putting together the computerised nostalgia jigsaw was CGI specialist Steven Wheeler, of Absolute Imaging.

He recalled: "It was quite time-consuming, but I enjoyed being able to create things with the help of a computer which you can't go out and simply film.

"We made use of archive footage, but we were so grateful to Liverpool Museums for giving us

access to Number 3 Carriage which actually ran on the Overhead Railway. We wanted to get as much historical accuracy as possible."

They did. And the affection for the Overhead Railway will always remain.

I may never have travelled along the famous railway. But now I know how it must have felt for those lucky to have experienced it. Usually you cannot get back to a place or a time but a piece if history awaits – a free ticket to glide . . . back into history.

The Liverpool Overhead Railway carriage passes the Three Graces on its way to the Museum of Liverpool at Mann Island

ing motor coach of the
head Railway (1893-1956)   Museum of Liverpool   NATIONAL MUSEUMS LIVERPOOL   Patton HERITAGE

SECURITY

In the Museum of Liverpool you will find out why and how the railway was built in 1893, meeting some of the people who worked and travelled on it along the way. You can climb aboard the carriage, which is fixed at the exact height of the original railway at 4.8m (16 feet) above the ground

GREAT READS FROM THE HEART OF THE CITY

THE LOST TRIBE OF EVERTON & SCOTTIE ROAD

This nostalgic book by Ken Rogers will take you back 'home' into the inner city streets and make you feel proud

NOW £8.00 +£1.50 p&p (UK)

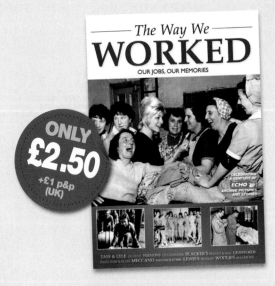

ONLY £2.50 +£1 p&p (UK)

THE WAY WE WORKED

Unilever, Vernons, Littlewoods, Crawford's, Tate & Lyle, Woolies. Our jobs – our memories

NEW BRIGHTON OUR DAYS OUT REMEMBERED

Recall magical childhood summers of the golden era of what was the greatest seaside resort in the whole world

ONLY £3.99 +£1.50 p&p (UK)

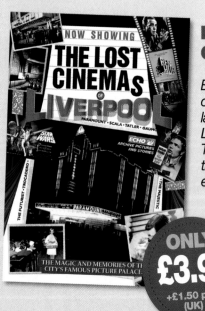

LOST CINEMAS OF LIVERPOOL

Book your ticket for a trip down movie memory lane, to a time when Liverpool was a Tinsel Town in its own right and there was a cinema on every corner

ONLY £3.99 +£1.50 p&p (UK)

ONLY £3.99 +£1.50 p&p (UK)

MERSEY FERRY TALES

A ticket to ride on the world's most famous ferry – a unique collection of magic maritime memories

* Offers while stocks last. Prices subject to change. Please telephone for international shipping rates.

100 YEARS OF THE LIVER BIRDS

Born in 1911 the Liver Birds are celebrating 100 years perched high over Liverpool looking into the city and out across the Mersey. A century of memories

ONLY £3.99
+£1.50 p&p
(UK)

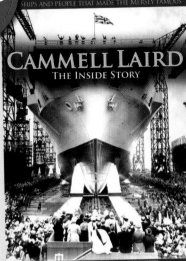

CAMMELL LAIRD
THE INSIDE STORY

The magic and memories of the world-famous shipbuilding company, told by Harry McLeish, a proud Lairdsman of 45 years

ONLY £3.99
+£1.50 p&p
(UK)

QUEENS OF THE MERSEY

Celebrating the historic visits of Cunard's Queen Elizabeth and Queen Mary 2 ocean liners to Liverpool

ONLY £3.99
+£1.50 p&p
(UK)

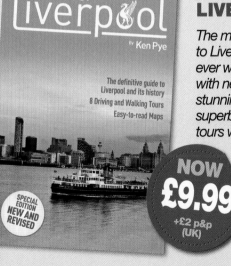

DISCOVER LIVERPOOL

The most definitive guide to Liverpool and its history, ever written – now updated with new information and stunning images. Features 8 superb driving and walking tours with maps.

NOW £9.99
+£2 p&p
(UK)

LIVERPOOL THEN: VOL 2

Flick back through a photo album that belongs to us all. An award-winning picture collection for generations to keep

ONLY £3.99
+ £1 p&p
(UK)

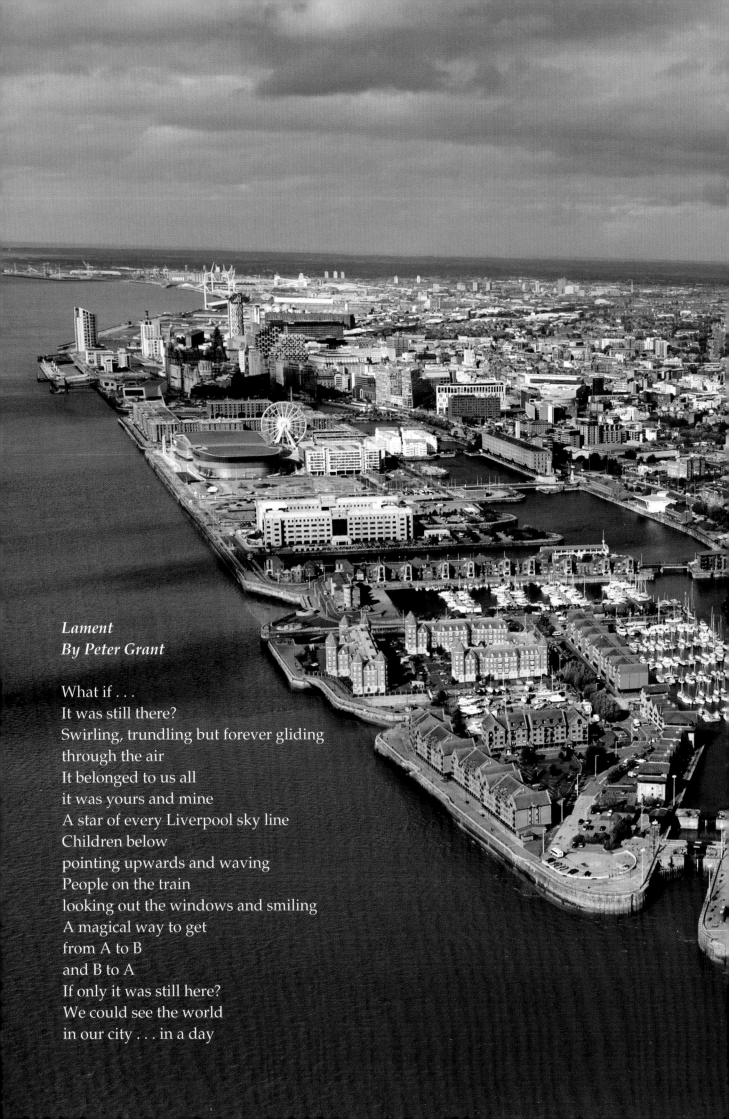

Lament
By Peter Grant

What if . . .
It was still there?
Swirling, trundling but forever gliding
through the air
It belonged to us all
it was yours and mine
A star of every Liverpool sky line
Children below
pointing upwards and waving
People on the train
looking out the windows and smiling
A magical way to get
from A to B
and B to A
If only it was still here?
We could see the world
in our city . . . in a day